artworld

What Is

GOTHIC ART?

by Kate Riggs

CREATIVE EDUCATION · CREATIVE PAPERBACKS

Published by Creative Education and Creative Paperbacks
P.O. Box 227, Mankato, Minnesota 56002
Creative Education and Creative Paperbacks are
imprints of The Creative Company
www.thecreativecompany.us

Design and production by Chelsey Luther
Art direction by Rita Marshall
Printed in the United States of America

Photographs by The Bridgeman Art Library (Nicolas Bataille/Musee des
Tapisseries, Angers, France/Bridgeman Images; Giotto di Bondone/
San Francesco, Upper Church, Assisi, Italy/Bridgeman Images; Giotto di
Bondone/Scrovegni [Arena] Chapel, Padua, Italy/Bridgeman Images;
Simone Martini/Palazzo Pubblico, Siena, Italy/Bridgeman Images), Corbis
(Elio Ciol, Corbis, Leemage, Pawel Libera), Flickr (Allan Harris), Getty
Images (Master Mateo), Wikimedia Creative Commons (Lluís Borrassà/
Amadalvarez, Lluís Borrassà/DcoetzeeBot)

Photo from Flickr on p. 12 adjusted in Photoshop.

Library of Congress Cataloging-in-Publication Data
Riggs, Kate.
What is gothic art? / Kate Riggs.
p. cm. — (Art world)
Summary: With prompting questions and historical background, an
early reader comes face to face with famous works of Gothic art and is
encouraged to identify emotions and consider the stories told.
Includes bibliographical references and index.
ISBN 978-1-60818-625-9 (hardcover)
ISBN 978-1-62832-223-1 (pbk)
ISBN 978-1-56660-691-2 (eBook)
1. Art, Gothic—Juvenile literature. I. Title.

N6310.R54 2016
709.02'2—dc23   2015008500

CCSS: RI.1.1, 2, 3, 5, 6, 7; RI.2.1, 2, 3, 5, 6, 7; RI.3.1, 3, 5, 7; RF.1.1; RF.2.3, 4;
RF.3.3

First Edition HC
9 8 7 6 5 4 3 2 1
First Edition PBK
9 8 7 6 5 4 3 2 1

Contents

Lighting the World 4

Tall Churches 6

Stories without Words 8

Curtained Off 11

Living Stone 12

Close to Reality 15

Showing Tears 16

Gothic Art and You 19

Portrait of a Gothic Artist 21

Glossary 22

Read More   Websites 23

Index 24

Light and colors.

Lighting the World

Mysteries and shadows. What do you see in a sculpture or building? If you see a sad face made of stone or **stained glass** in a church, you may be looking at Gothic art.

Stained-glass windows in a Paris church

Tall Churches

From 1150 to 1400, people built large churches. They had pointed arches and tall windows. This time was called the Gothic.

People started building the Milan Cathedral in 1386.

Stories without Words

Colorful windows told stories from the Bible. Paintings called **frescoes** covered the walls. Many people did not know how to read. They learned the stories by looking at the pictures.

This fresco was painted on a government building in Italy.

Bataille wove stories from the Bible into cloth.

Curtained Off

Heavy curtains hung on cold, stone walls. Nicolas Bataille made one called "St. John Eating the Book" (1373–87). Look at the expression on John's face. He is eating the words an angel gave him.

Living Stone

Giovanni Pisano carved people and animals out of stone. He wanted to make them look alive. He carved flowing lines. He made people look sad or excited.

Pisano's stone carvings are found in Italian churches.

This piece is about the nativity, or birth, of Jesus.

Close to Reality

Pisano carved the story of Jesus's birth in stone. Look at all the people and angels in *Annunciation, Nativity, and Adoration of the Shepherds* (1297–1301). In the center is the baby Jesus. His mother reaches out her hand to him. It looks like she is tucking him in.

Showing Tears

Do you think angels can cry? Gothic artists wanted to show **emotions** in their work. Giotto (*JAH-toe*) painted a sad scene of Jesus's death. Some of the figures have their hands on their faces. Others have their arms pushed out.

The Lamentation (1305–06), by Giotto

Gothic statues were sometimes painted.

Gothic Art and You

What do you see in a Gothic work of art? Does it tell a story? Look around your town to find stories in stone!

Portrait of a Gothic Artist

Luis Borrassà was born near the end of the Gothic age. He came from northern Spain. Many of his paintings were for churches. They told stories of saints and people from the Bible.

Borrassà made works called altarpieces for Spanish churches.

Glossary

emotions—feelings such as happiness, sadness, fearfulness, and excitement

expression—the look on someone's face; expressions may be happy, sad, or another emotion

frescoes—paintings done on walls or ceilings made of plaster

saints—people known for their good deeds

stained glass—colored glass most often seen in church windows

Read More

Alexander, Heather. *A Child's Introduction to Art*. New York: Black Dog & Leventhal, 2014.

Raczka, Bob. *Name That Style: All about Isms in Art*. Minneapolis: Millbrook Press, 2009.

Websites

DLTK's Stained Glass Crafts
http://www.dltk-kids.com/type/stained-glass.htm
Make your own stained-glass windows using paper and other materials.

PBS Crafts for Kids
http://www.pbs.org/parents/crafts-for-kids/3d-art-projects/
Paint a picture that you can microwave and then hang on your wall!

NOTE: Every effort has been made to ensure that the websites listed above are suitable for children, that they have educational value, and that they contain no inappropriate material. However, because of the nature of the Internet, it is impossible to guarantee that these sites will remain active indefinitely or that their contents will not be altered.

Index

Bataille, Nicolas 11

Borrassà, Luis 21

churches 5, 6, 21

emotions 12, 16

frescoes 8

Giotto 16

Pisano, Giovanni 12, 15

sculptures 5, 12, 15

stained glass 5, 8

stories 8, 15, 19, 21

subjects 8, 11, 15, 16, 21